Teen Voices
Real Teens Discuss
Real Problems™

Teens Talk About
Drugs and
Alcohol

Edited by Jennifer Landau

Featuring Q&As with Teen Health & Wellness's Dr. Jan

Rosen
YA™
New York

Library of Congress Cataloging-in-Publication Data

Names: Landau, Jennifer, 1961– editor.
Title: Teens talk about drugs and alcohol / edited by Jennifer Landau.
Description: New York : Rosen Publishing, 2018 | Series: Teen voices: Real teens discuss real problems | Includes bibliographical references and index. | Audience: Grades 7–12.
Identifiers: LCCN 2017016028| ISBN 9781508176503 (library bound) | ISBN 9781508176589 (pbk.) | ISBN 9781508176343 (6 pack)
Subjects: LCSH: Teenagers—Alcohol use—Juvenile literature. | Teenagers—Drug use—Juvenile literature. | Children of alcoholics—Juvenile literature. | Children of drug addicts—Juvenile literature.
Classification: LCC HV5824.Y68 T45 2018 | DDC 362.290835—dc23
LC record available at https://lccn.loc.gov/2017016028

Manufactured in China

The content in this title has been compiled from The Rosen Publishing Group's Teen Health & Wellness digital platform. Additional original content was provided by Barbara Gottfried Hollander.

Contents

Introduction

Do you live with an addicted parent? Have you ever seen your parent lose control from drug or alcohol abuse? There are ways to protect yourself when addicted parents become violent or verbally confrontational. How can you or a friend from a home with addiction move on to lead a functional adult life without becoming an addict, too? Children of addicts grow up deprived of basic physical and psychological needs, but they can learn to make healthier choices with appropriate support.

According to the Substance Abuse and Mental Health Services Administration (SAMHSA), about 12 percent of children live with a substance-abusing parent, with alcohol being the most commonly abused substance. Between 2011 and 2012, SAMHSA also found that nearly 18.3 percent of pregnant women between the ages of fifteen and seventeen used substances, putting their children at risk for developmental delays or even death. In *The Mystery of Risk: Drugs, Alcohol, Pregnancy, and the Vulnerable Child*, Ira J. Chasnoff notes that some studies report

Addiction can be the cause of many family fights, whether the addict is a parent, a sibling, or even you.

that close to 30 percent of babies are exposed to drugs or alcohol before they are even born.

Living with a family member or having a friend that abuses drugs or alcohol hurts. It forces children to grow up quickly, make tough choices, and work through painful situations. It often requires children to be caregivers for their parents or siblings, without having the opportunities to develop proper tools for these roles. All of these hardships are made even more difficult when family members of addicts face physical and emotional challenges, which can often result from living with someone addicted to alcohol or drugs.

Share Your Own Story

The stories you are about to read were submitted by your peers to the Teen Health & Wellness Personal Story Project. Sharing stories is a powerful way to connect with other people. By sharing your story, you can connect with others who are dealing with these challenges. Find more information about how to submit your own story at the end of this resource.

Sometimes, the addict in the house is the teen. According to the Center on Addiction and Substance Abuse at Columbia University, forty million addicts in the United States are age twelve and older. The SAMHSA's National Survey on Drug Use reports that in 2014 twenty-seven million people in this age group had used illicit drugs or illegal drugs taken for non-medical purposes. Drug and alcohol abuse is also associated with teen suicides. According to a 2016 report by the Canadian Centre on Substance Abuse, alcohol abuse was seven and half times higher in teens who died by suicide than in the community control group and illicit drug abuse was nine times higher.

Some drug use can be beneficial, like taking an antibiotic to treat an ear infection. Many people do use legal drugs responsibly to achieve intended results. But sometimes, drug use becomes drug abuse. Abuse occurs when a person uses something or someone in an unhealthy way, despite the harmful consequences.

Some addicts begin by taking prescription drugs for beneficial reasons, but then develop an addiction to these medications.

For example, drug or alcohol addicts continue abusing substances even when it causes themselves and others harm.

Do you know someone who abuses drugs, like marijuana, cocaine, tobacco, or inhalants? Does someone close to you have an alcohol addiction? Has a friend or relative been abusing prescription drugs? Are you an addict yourself? Family members or friends of addicts, as well as recovering addicts, can learn the tools needed to heal and lead healthier lives. There are programs such as Alcoholics Anonymous and Al-Anon that help addicts and their families deal with the challenges brought about by addiction. Addiction recovery involves a plan aimed at preventing relapses and a lifetime commitment to stop abusing drugs or alcohol. Psychotherapy and psychiatric medications may also be part of that plan. With help, the cycle of addiction can be stopped.

Chapter 1

Teens Talk About Drinking and Driving

Many teens have been in cars with drunk drivers— maybe, they were the ones driving drunk. According to the National Highway Traffic Safety Administration (NHTSA) twenty-eight people die from drunk driving-related accidents every day—one death every fifty-three minutes. The NHTSA also reports that on average, two out of three people will be involved in alcohol-related crashes during their lives.

Reckless driving can alert police officers to drunk drivers. Running stop signs or red lights, speeding, swerving, and even failing to signal are reasons to pull a driver over. Certain physical tests (like asking a driver to walk a straight line) and/or chemical tests (such as checking a driver's breath, blood, or urine for alcohol) may be used to determine if a driver is drunk. For example, a driver is classified as drunk if his or her blood alcohol content (BAC) is greater than 0.08 percent. For an average-size person, this legal limit can be exceeded with three to four drinks.

Driving under the influence of alcohol or drugs can lead to car accidents, which may result in injuries, deaths, and property damage.

Drunk drivers face losing their licenses, incurring fines, and being arrested. Since the minimum drinking age in the United States is twenty-one, drunk teen drivers also face the penalties of having illegally consumed alcohol. Drunk driving can cause death, injuries to surviving victims, and property damage. The best way to avoid these serious consequences is to not drink and drive.

Preston's Story

"We should not look back unless it is to derive useful lessons from past errors, and for the purpose of profiting by dearly bought experience."
—George Washington.

I couldn't agree more with Washington's words about learning from our own dumb mistakes. We all think we know everything when we are young and that we clearly understand the choices we make. I was wrong in many ways because I made the choice to drink and drive. We all think we can because we are able to walk and talk right, but the truth is, we can't. And even thinking we're able to makes us immature and cocky in so many ways. This all began last summer, when I was about to go into my senior year of high school. However, I chose to drink and drive under the influence of alcohol. Though it may sound like it's not a big deal, it is. Now I am living with the consequences.

It started out with a couple of friends and me grilling out. We were just having a good time and thinking life couldn't get any better. After we ate and swam, another friend came over with a couple cases of Bud Light and malt drinks. We didn't stop until most of us couldn't walk or keep an intelligent conversation going. But I happened to be the least intoxicated one out of the four of us. Later that night we were invited to a party, which was just down the road. We walked there, but I was so drunk I wasn't really able to walk.

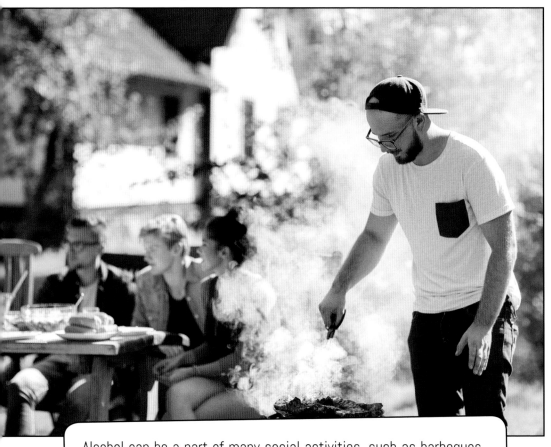

Alcohol can be a part of many social activities, such as barbeques and parties. Making responsible drinking decisions when at these events can save lives.

After the party, we went back to my friend's house and decided that I would drive us to get milkshakes from Whataburger. We got into my truck, which was the mistake that would change my ways and how I looked at young adults and drinking alcohol as a whole. Right after making an illegal U-turn, I was pulled over by a Dallas police officer. From there, he did the normal "license and registration, please." I gave it to him. He came back to my window and asked if I had been

Police officers use breathalyzers to determine the amount of blood alcohol content (BAC) in drunk-driving suspects. This test detects the alcohol concentration that has passed through the lungs' air

drinking. In this situation most people would say no, but cops aren't stupid. I told him yes, thinking he wouldn't take me to jail.

Fortunately, saying yes to that and being respectful to the officer kept me from going to jail that night. But it wasn't over yet. He asked me to step out of the vehicle and gave me the field sobriety test, which I failed with a BAC of just under .08. Because I was under 21 it didn't matter that I was under the limit—I shouldn't have had any alcohol in my system. He then went to everyone in my truck and tested them, as well. After talking to the officer, he told us he could either take me downtown or have somebody come pick us up. I could tell that he didn't want to take us downtown, though. So my friend called his soccer coach to come and drive my truck back to the house where we were staying. On the way home it didn't really occur to me what had just happened because I was still under the influence.

Being honest with parents or other caregivers about your drinking or drug use can be an important first step toward getting the help you need.

However, once morning came around I finally realized what had happened the night before and how big of a deal this was going to turn out to be. I got up, headed over to my house, and explained to my parents what happened. At first it took me almost fifteen minutes to have enough courage to tell them about my infraction, rather than beating around the bush and not telling them the exact details. They told me to let this be a life lesson because later in life if you repeat a mistake or have the same issue, it will be more serious and costly and will cause you to have major issues later in life. Then, I wouldn't be able to turn the clock around.

My advice is to wait until you're of legal age to drink, if you are going to, and if you need to get home take a cab to save your own life and somebody else's. You don't need that to be on your conscience.

MYTHS **AND** FACTS

MYTH   Drunk driving is not a leading killer of
       young Americans.

FACT   The NHTSA reports that drunk driving is the
       number one killer of Americans between the
       ages of fifteen and twenty years.

MYTH   After consuming a few beers, a person can sober
       up by sleeping for an hour or having one cup of
       coffee before driving.

FACT   It takes about two hours to metabolize one
       standard serving of alcohol, such as a can
       of beer.

MYTH   A person can only be charged with driving under
       the influence (DUI) while driving a car.

FACT   In some states, people no longer in their cars
       are charged with DUIs for being drunk if a police
       officer believes they were recently driving.

Chapter 2

Teens Talk About Friends Who Abuse Drugs and Alcohol

Being friends with someone who abuses drugs and alcohol is difficult. Friends want to help each other, but there is a difference between enabling and helping. Enabling includes misguided attempts to help a substance abuser. It limits the consequences of a person's actions. Suppose a parent finds Ecstasy in her son's room and suspects her son is abusing drugs. The son's friend lies and says that the drugs belong to him. As a result, the parent drops the issue. The friend thinks his actions helped his buddy stay out of trouble. In reality, his actions enabled that person to continue abusing drugs.

Substance abusers can be a bad influence on their friends. They might try to pressure the friend into abusing drugs, too. Addicts can put their friends in risky situations, such as being questioned by the police or being exposed to other drug addicts. A substance abuser can also directly hurt his or her friends by

Relationships with people who abuse alcohol or drugs are complicated and often unhealthy. It can be hard to draw the line between supporting a friend and knowing when to let go.

stealing, lying, and even becoming physically aggressive toward them. Being friends with a substance abuser means taking a long, hard look at the consequences of the relationship and sometimes deciding to let go.

A person cannot fix a friend's drug or alcohol-related problems. An addict must acknowledge the addiction, its consequences, and the need for recovery. The

When an addict takes ownership of his or her dependence on drugs or alcohol, friends can be part of the support system that helps the addict down a path toward recovery.

responsibility for these steps lies with the addict—not the friend or relative of the addict. After the addict seeks help, friends and family can then choose to be part of the support system. This help may include active listening, which means giving the speaker your full concentration. Other ways to help are by doing substance-free activities together and encouraging the addict to participate in recovery-related support groups.

An unhealthy peer group can lead to, or reinforce, drug and alcohol addiction. Losing one's ability to feel close to friends hurts the addict's chances of recovery.

Ben's Story

One of the biggest mistakes, and yet one of the most beneficial experiences, of my life was choosing to spend my time with the friends I had in the second half of high school. The people in this circle of friends smoked marijuana and drank alcohol frequently, did not care about school, and, worst of all, were terribly selfish. These were the kind of people who would take

Making healthy decisions regarding drug and alcohol use often leads to more positive relationships and greater academic and work opportunities.

advantage of and lie to their closest "friends." I spent my time with these people largely because of the death of my father. At a time when I had lost my sense of self they seemingly provided a refuge from my grief.

Eventually, though, I was able to see the mistake I had made. From the experience I learned that nothing is gained from apathy toward learning. I now take a great deal of enjoyment from school and pushing my intellectual capabilities. I also found that there is no reason to associate with people who care only about themselves. Once I made these realizations I distanced myself from these friends. After realizing I needed to spend my time with genuinely good people, I was able to connect with some schoolmates who are some of my best friends to this day. I essentially went from defining myself in ways that were counterproductive and untrue to my character to beginning the path to becoming the person I believe I ought to be.

Michael's Story

When I was about ten years old, I was like everyone else. I had my own little group of friends. We all would hang out together and have fun. But I never really had that one best friend, the one who you could hang out with forever and never get sick of. That all changed when I met Cameron. From the very beginning, we clicked like best friends do. We liked all the same games, had the same sense of humor, and soon became inseparable. We had been best friends for about a year when things started to get really bad for him. His parents

Troubled relationships, especially those that involve conflict and manipulation, hurt both the addict and the people in his or her life.

got divorced, eventually got back together, and then divorced again. His mother got heavily involved in drugs and alcohol and fell into such a deep depression that it was rare for her to even get out of bed.

At this point, I knew that he was going to need his friends more than ever. His mom would tell him that he needed to go find a place to stay. He would stay at our house for weeks. We became family. I considered him my little brother because we had been through so much together. My parents weren't too supportive of Cameron staying at our house, mostly because they were mad at his mother for forcing them to pretty much take in and support another child. They let him stay because he literally had no other place to go. And they couldn't let him live on the streets.

We were best friend for five years. But as we hit high school, we slowly began to go our separate ways. The time between hanging out would grow from weeks, to months, eventually to the point where I didn't see him for a whole year. Then out of the blue he showed up, looking and acting completely different. I asked him how he was and if he wanted to go find something to do. He said he couldn't because he was living with his dad now and he was grounded. I of course asked him why. He nonchalantly told me that his dad had found drugs in his room.

I was shocked to learn this, but that was not even him hitting rock bottom. A few weeks later we found out that he had broken into our house and taken our computers and Xbox. He got away and went to some town that I had never even heard of before. The items were easily replaced, but all of this hit me like a bomb.

I couldn't figure out how my best friend, the person I looked at as my little brother, could do something like this to me. How could he completely turn on me like this? How could he hurt the family that picked him up when he was completely knocked down? I then started to feel guilty, as if he did this because I turned my back

People with friends who are addicts can experience many negative emotions, including depression, anger, guilt, and fear.

on him. I ditched him for the friends at my school, and I wasn't there to watch over him and make sure he stayed on a straight path. Was it my fault that he became a druggy and a thief?

I eventually came to the realization that it was not my fault. It was not my job to watch him and make sure that he would stay out of trouble all the time. I was not his mother. Although I still feel bad that things did not turn out differently, I know that I have to go my own way, live my own life, and make my own friends.

Ask Dr. Jan

Dear Dr. Jan,
My father drinks a lot at home and I think he could be an alcoholic. Sometimes he drives when he's drunk even though he knows it is against the law. How can I get him to stop?
— Sean

Dear Sean,
Unfortunately, alcohol is one of the most addictive drugs on the planet. If your dad is an alcoholic, he may need to get help in order to address his drinking. As with many addictions, it can be very difficult at first to get the substance user to acknowledge he has a problem and then participate in treatment. You should also know that the chances that a child will become an alcoholic increase if a parent suffers from alcoholism. So, if you are correct about your dad, you and your siblings would be wise to avoid drinking alcohol altogether.

In response to your question, unfortunately you cannot get your dad to stop drinking unless he is willing to try to change his behavior. What you can do is let him know that you love him and are concerned for his safety and the safety of your family members when he drives under the influence of alcohol.

If that would be too difficult, it might be best to first have the conversation with your mom about the best way to approach your dad about his drinking. If that is not possible, it may be helpful to speak to a trusted adult (e.g., school staff, a relative, or family friend). Sometimes families will organize an "intervention": they plan a meeting with a group of family members and friends to confront the substance abuser with their concerns, if they have already tried in vain to talk to him or her individually. It is often useful to have a mental health professional, with expertise in addiction issues, present to help lead the intervention.

If all of this fails, families then have to take the difficult step of getting the police involved. Once a driver gets arrested for driving while intoxicated, the courts often mandate substance abuse treatment. While these steps are very difficult, it would be far worse for your dad, a family member, and/or an innocent bystander to get hurt or killed before something is done about it. I would also encourage you (and your family) to refuse to get in the car if your dad has been drinking.

Chapter 3

Teens Talk About Having an Alcoholic Family Member

The actions of addicts affect their families. Many addicts cannot provide basic physical needs for their families, such as food, clothing, and shelter. Their addictions also hinder them from fulfilling psychological needs, such as making children feel secure, loved, and valued. Children of addicts are often neglected or abused. They experience high levels of stress and bear the burden of caring for their addicted parents and suffering siblings. Children of alcoholics are also more likely to become alcoholics themselves.

A pregnant addict can harm her infant child in the womb. Her substance abuse can result in birth defects and developmental delays. The most serious fetal alcohol spectrum disorder (FASDs) is fetal alcohol syndrome (FAS). Babies with FAS may experience seizures; heart, bone, and kidney problems; hearing

Children of alcoholics not only suffer through the effects of their parents' addictions, but also carry the risk of following in their parents' footsteps and become addicts themselves.

and vision issues; and challenges with weight gain and behavior. Before a child even enters the world, he or she is hurt by addiction.

Family members often suffer due to an alcoholic's erratic and dangerous behaviors, which can include violent outbursts, constant arguments, and abandonment. Children of alcoholics are at risk for developing mental health issues, such as depression and anxiety disorders. They are often fearful of losing control, expressing feelings, intimacy, and conflicts. At other times, they seek out chaotic situations because they are familiar to them.

Children of alcoholics may even develop post-traumatic stress disorder (PTSD) from traumas inflicted on them directly or indirectly by their alcoholic family members. Symptoms of PTSD include experiencing flashbacks to a traumatic event, having recurring bad dreams, and physical symptoms such as a racing heart or excessive sweating. Teens can address PTSD in numerous ways, such as undergoing psychotherapy, practicing relaxation techniques like meditation and yoga, engaging in artistic or athletic activities, and taking antidepressants or anti-anxiety medications.

Whitney's Story

Every night I would sit there and watch as they filled up their glasses again. By that time, I had usually lost count on how many glasses they had already drunk. During the day, they were the happy parents I loved. We would have conversations about life and school, but every night around five I'd hear the wine bottle coming out of the fridge. I would sit on the couch and watch as my parents smiled and laughed, knowing that in about two hours they would hate each other and have another argument. At home there are my parents, my two sisters, and me. One sister is close to my age and the other is four years older. My oldest sister has autism and major panic attacks. When my parents started to argue, I had to be the one to calm my older sister down. I had

The burdens of being a child of an alcoholic include caring for siblings, and performing household duties that are usually the responsibility of the parent.

to be the mature adult in the family when the actual adults were too drunk to even notice they were scaring my sister.

The only times they didn't drink and then argue was when they would have to work in the morning. I loved those days so much. When they had to work in the morning, they couldn't stay up all night yelling. On the other nights, I would lie awake at night and stare at the ceiling, listening to my parents scream at each other. When I'd look over at my younger sister lying beside me, I knew she was still awake and listening, too.

I'd get mad when I saw my mom or dad with a glass of alcohol in their hands. I'd get mad when they argued because I knew there was nothing I could do to stop them. I'd get mad when I saw my autistic sister run to me just so I could tell her it's okay. I'd get mad when I watched as my autistic sister tried to stop my parents from arguing. I would watch as she stood outside their bedroom door with her hands covering her ears as she cried. My younger sister, however, learned how to block it out. I watched her continue reading or continue watching TV when my parents were screaming at each other. The only way I knew how to deal with it was to continue on with what I was doing and try to ignore them the best I could.

Sometimes I would phone my eldest sister, who is thirteen years older, because she also remembers what it was like. Whenever I would talk to her, she would comfort me. She would give me words of advice and tell me to "just keep swimming." I knew that she understood what my other sisters and I were going through almost every night. My parents, of course, never got into physical arguments. They just had the type where you yell and scream at each other for most of the night.

What I have learned about myself throughout the years is that when my parents drank and fought, I felt like I had to be more mature than I really was. The best thing I ever did during this whole situation was talk to my parents. My sisters and I held an intervention. We took my parents and made them sit on the couch. Then we each took a turn talking to my parents and telling them how we felt. Now my parents don't drink as much and the arguing has slowed down. I will admit they haven't completely stopped arguing, but it has become less frequent. In the end, no matter what my parents argue about or what my sisters and I had to go through (and some nights still do), I love my family and I wouldn't ask for any other parents.

Jaquetta's Story

When one thinks of a problem concerning teens, it is usually considered child's play or a situation that is significantly overdramatized. These scenarios include: relationship problems, bullying, body image issues, peer pressure, and drugs. It is an outrage that as teens our situations are merely pushed to the side and not treated as important by "grown-ups," who face "real" problems such as financial trouble and stress. Newsflash: adults are not the only ones whose problems create long-term pain and suffering. As teens we have often heard the line "been there, done that" from many of our

Having a creative outlet can help teens with addicted family members express their feelings, and may even inspire them to share those feelings with others.

older relatives who strive to assure us our problems are not as difficult as they may seem. But they don't understand that not everyone can handle the same amount of pain or suffering. We may be teens who do encounter petty situations like misplacing our favorite sweater or breaking a nail, but we are victims as well. Victims of unbearable amounts of pain, grief, and heartbreak. These internal struggles are struggles that cannot be explained through basic communication, so we try to express them through music, writing, art, and in the most unfortunate cases, suicide notes. It's time someone listened.

Despite my adolescence, I have not encountered many of the stereotypical disturbances associated with being young, wild, and free. I've had my heart broken, but not by a significant other. I've had body image issues, but as of now they are in the past and the least of my worries. What I am here to discuss is the unbearable debt that death has not only on adults, but also on adolescents. Yes, I am here to discuss one of life's most unfortunate series of events. It is a topic no one likes to talk about, but to help someone who desperately needs guidance I will take my chances.

At the age of five a child should be happy and full of life, looking forward to every adventure that lies just around the corner. I was all of these things and a bit more. Despite my strenuous family situation when my mother and father separated, I found means to be happy. I spent most of my time at my mother's home, but my father's house was my fortress. It was where I found things to do in nature. I would take walks and play in his dirt-filled yard. Those days were the best days of my childhood. Those days tragically came to an end when my father passed away. He wasn't sick or anything, but he was an alcoholic. Despite the negative connotation directed toward alcoholic parents, my father was a great man. He never drank around my older brother and me; or maybe he did and I wasn't aware. Those brown paper bags were a mystery then.

After my father passed away, everything went downhill. Even now as I strive to rid myself of my horrible past, I find myself rigid with anger. This anger is directed toward no one in particular, but it affects everyone. After my father passed away, my mother began to struggle emotionally and financially. She was already suffering because my grandmother, whose health had been rapidly deteriorating, had died not long before my father died. I felt lost and unmistakably alone. I went into a state of pure hatred as I became older, tearing my father's picture off of my wall and cursing him for leaving me to face the inevitable alone. My mother didn't understand my anger. She thought it wasn't the typical reaction to the loss of a parent as it was completely opposite to her reaction to losing her mother. I couldn't explain it, either. I was always Daddy's little girl, but how can you be Daddy's little girl without Daddy?

Soon, I would go on a journey of enlightenment. After the self-diagnosed depression and constant negativity, I began to realize the power I had within myself. Initially believing that being without my father was a downfall, I began to realize that I was forced to become independent because he wasn't there. As a young person I was able to promptly make appropriate decisions, because I wanted to make my father proud and make sure his death was not in vain. Therefore, I was forced to gain specific knowledge and teach myself the ways of the world so that I may grow into someone worthy of respect.

I generally refer to myself as the one who got away because, when people think of a young girl growing up without a father figure, they think of someone who is promiscuous and easily manipulated since her father is

Sometimes healing involves coming to terms with the actions of an alcoholic parent after he or she dies, and strengthening the relationship with the surviving parent.

not there to explain the birds and the bees. Sure, she has a mother, but she is never the same with one half missing. I am proof that this stereotype is exactly that: a stereotype. I became a person who decided to share her story in an attempt to help others with the unbearable void of a missing parent.

It isn't the end. You don't have to be angry or view yourself as someone who is less fortunate. Take your experience and use it as fuel for your fire. Share your story so that others may know it is possible to live (and live happily) after a parent dies. Follow every dream you've ever had, knowing that the parent you have lost will be proud. In turn, express gratitude for the parent who is still there. Let them be your shoulder to lean on. Tell them how you feel and share your pain. Remember the good times and you will laugh together, and together you will know that the death of your loved one was not in vain. My mother is standing over my shoulder, smiling as I type these last words.

Zachary's Story

I love to spend time with my family during holidays. We all like to go to my grandparents' house to eat a delicious meal with my cousins. Most of my favorite memories come from these occasions. I get to see all of my family on a regular basis, except for my grandpa.

My grandpa lives far away from us, but that is not the problem. He is an alcoholic. My mom tries to keep us away from him as much as possible. Every time we do get to go see him, my mom has to call early that

Initial treatment for a recovering addict can include time at a rehabilitation center. But an addict also needs to make a lifetime commitment to remaining sober.

morning to make sure that he does not drink at all that day. Even when we do go and see him, we only get to spend a small amount of time with him. He can barely stand to go an hour without having a drink. This makes my family very sad, but most of all it tears my mother's heart apart. She has been affected by his drinking her whole life.

A couple of years ago, we confronted him with his problems. We asked him if he wanted to go to a rehabilitation center in Florida. Our whole family stood up and read some letters to him to express our opinions. My letter said:

Dear Grandpa,
I love to spend time with you. I really like to come over to your house and go fishing. My best moments come from our turkey hunts together. I remember that the first time I ever drove a car I was nine years old and I was in your truck. These moments are always great. The only problem is that we cannot do all of this anymore because your drinking has gotten way to out of hand. I would really like to spend more time with you, and I would like you to be healthy more than anything.

I love you Grandpa,
Zachary

He accepted our offer and he went to the rehabilitation center. Our family wished him good luck on his battle through alcoholism. He went away for about three months and came back alcohol-free. Our family was very happy for him, and we were glad to have him back home. We heard less than a month later that he was back on his drinking. My mom still won't let us go see him that much.

I have noticed that my mother's drinking has increased in the past couple of years. I went up to her and said, "Mom, your drinking has increased recently. Is this because of Grandpa?" She said, "No, it's just something that adults do for fun."

I know that she is afraid to admit it, but I still think that she is stressed about it. I told her, "Drinking is not only making this situation worse, but it is also turning you into him." Sometimes she asks me to go and get her some 7-Up for her alcohol. I tell her that I will not do anything to help her drink. I have made it my goal to help do whatever I can to prevent anybody I know from becoming an alcoholic. I am not able to see my grandpa because of the choices he made with his life, and I do not want it to be the same with my mom.

Aden's Story

"Please help me," he begs.

It's minutes to midnight and I'm holding back tears. Poorly concealed blotches of red and purple—no doubt the aftermath of his father's drunken stupor—dot my student's skin. With his head buried between his marred arms, he begs, "Please." My heart bleeds.

Three years ago, I was in his shoes.

I can still remember the crunch of breaking glass beneath my father's boots, the pungent odor of Smirnoff on his breath, and the hours I spent with my head tucked between my knees, feebly whispering, "I'm okay, I'm okay." I could not survive there. I had to leave, so without looking at my father—the man who raised me—I walked out.

I scrambled to pay rent, dismissing hang-out invitations to work as a Taekwondo instructor and a photographer. While other runaways loitered in shady corner delis to smoke, I spent my after-school hours

Serving as a teacher or mentor to a younger child can build up the self-esteem of a teen who has survived abuse at the hands of an addicted parent.

teaching not only self-defense, but also the importance of appreciation. It brought a lump to my throat to see Matteo, a four-year-old greenbelt, say, "Thank you Mommy," or Aidan, my six year old protégé, whisper, "I love you Daddy." When not at Taekwondo, I expanded my photography portfolio, capturing happy moments I wished I could've shared. Only after juggling two jobs did I finally, much to my landlord's satisfaction, earn enough to scrape by.

Rent exhausted my income. Living in an impoverished room, I wore ripped jeans and tattered jackets and carried around a broken bag. Every last penny went to food, rent, and my college fund. Even though I had neither a tree nor gifts, I was content to spend my Christmas alone listening to "Frosty the Snowman" and reading holiday cards. On my birthday, I indulged in a small cake—my one and only treat—before putting on my frayed winter coat and leaving for Taekwondo.

Worse than celebrating alone was hearing people say, "Your parents must be so proud." That praise was wasted on me. I spent so many nights tossing and turning, pondering where I went wrong. How could my father—how could any father—hurt his son without reason? But perhaps a better question would've been: why did I need to know so badly?

I didn't.

Despite my lack of clarity, I gritted my teeth and convinced myself that the question "why" shouldn't matter. I chose not to dwell. Instead, I focused on handling school, Taekwondo, and photography, ensuring that in a few years I wouldn't have to look back and regret.

That's why I'm here watching my student bury his head between his knees as I imagine him whispering to himself, "I'm okay, I'm okay?" and wondering if he is also haunted by the scent of booze and the sound of

Who to Call

The following hotlines and organizations offer support to teens dealing with issues related to alcoholism and drug abuse:

Al-Anon/Alateen
888-425-2666
http://www.al-anon.alateen.org
8 am to 6 pm EST, Monday to Friday

Crisis Call Center
800-273-8255 or text ANSWER to 839863
http://crisiscallcenter.org/crisis-services
Twenty-four hours a day, seven days a week

The National Alcohol and Substance Abuse Information Center
800-784-6776
http://www.addictioncareoptions.com
Twenty-four hours a day, seven days a week

National Institute on Alcohol Abuse and Alcoholism
800-662-HELP
http://www.niaaa.nih.gov
Twenty-four hours a day, seven days a week

glass crunching underfoot. My tears trickle downward as I roll up my sleeves. He looks up, reaches forward, and traces the lines etched into my skin: the scars that so perfectly match his.

"You too," he says.

Yes, me too. But now I know we're not alone and that we never were. Thousands are still fighting, trying to make sense of everything, believing that if they can find the cause, they can find their way out. But I learned alongside my student that when troubles come, it's not our job to find fault or a reason, but instead to learn and move on. Because I survived, I know that my dreams of university, a family, and success are still conceivable. Everything leading up to this point has been a test of my resolve. I'm fighting for my dreams. I want to prove to others that they are still within my reach.

For them, I want to succeed.

And for myself, I need to succeed.

Chapter 4

Teens Talk About Having a Drug-Addicted Family Member

More people die from drug overdoses than from car accidents. In 2016, the Centers for Disease Control and Prevention (CDC) reported that from 2000 to 2015 ninety-one people died every day in the United States from an opioid overdose. Opioids are drugs that relieve pain by acting on the nervous system. This class of drugs includes methadone, oxycodone, hydrocodone, morphine, and codeine.

People also abuse Attention Deficit Hyperactivity Disorder (ADHD) medications and anxiety-reducing depressants (such as Valium). According to SAMHSA's National Survey on Drug Use and Health, the abuse of prescription drugs in the United States is becoming increasingly prevalent, with many people getting these drugs from a friend or relative for free. Doctors prescribe medications to treat their patients—these drugs are not meant to be shared.

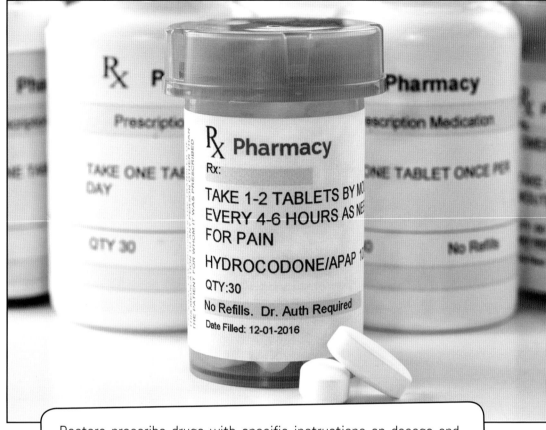

Doctors prescribe drugs with specific instructions on dosage and frequency. Taking the drugs at higher dosages and more often than the doctor directed can put you at risk for addiction.

While the use of illicit drugs, prescription narcotics and amphetamines, and heroin have decreased in recent decades, drug abuse remains a challenge faced by many children in their homes. They grow up with the devastating effects of having drug addicts in their families, often feeling shame, helplessness, sadness, anger, and fear. They must also face disappointment when the addict continually breaks promises, such as not showing up for prearranged visits or events.

Drug abuse affects people of all ages and backgrounds. Children of addicts can live chaotic lives, filled with neglect and abuse. It is difficult for young children and teens to understand and cope with their family members's drug addictions. Teens from families with addiction also have a higher rate of becoming addicts themselves. But the tools to recover from drug abuse and to resist becoming an addict do exist, as does a better life free from the harmful effects of addiction.

Mercedes's Story

Congratulations! You've been dealt a hand of playing cards. These cards are not normal cards. They tell you the different challenges you will go through in life. Look down and see what you have been given. For me, my cards tell me I've been adopted, and I won't ever know my "real" mom.

This is where my story begins. My biological mom was addicted to drugs and alcohol. When I was in her womb, she continued her need or addiction for drugs. Her main drug of choice was meth. Once she gave birth to me and I was able to go home (it took awhile since I had a small case of Fetal Alcohol Syndrome), I was put into a foster home.

During this time my biological mom could come visit me, if she wanted. She used to set up the visits, but at the last minute would make up an excuse as to why she couldn't come. By the time I was three, my foster mom had had enough of my biological mom disappointing me, so she adopted me. Around the time she adopted me, my biological mom was sent to prison for drugs.

How did this set me up in life? I have the obvious faults that come with this situation, which are FASD and a tendency toward addiction to harmful substances. Then there are the not so obvious ones: growing up thinking that my biological family and mom didn't want anything to do with me. Also, there is the feeling of not fitting in with the family that I live with now. These things helped mold my life; they made me who I am today. Now I've been living this life for seventeen years. Look at how I've dealt with it: yes I have pink hair, piercings, tight pants, and scars on my wrist, but I've also got a family who loves me. Most importantly I haven't given up on myself. Sure there were those days when I would just say "screw it, nothing matters anymore." You've got to remember though, all that matters is how you handle the things that are handed to you.

I've been given these challenges for a reason. These cards help form my life, for good or for bad. The choice is mine. All I've got to do is learn how to play my cards right. There is nothing in life that I can't handle and nothing that I cannot accomplish. If I put my all into it, it will make me great. Greater than I already am.

10 Great Questions
to Ask a Drug and Alcohol Counselor

1. How can I tell if a friend or relative has a drug or alcohol addiction?

2. How can I help my addicted parent or friend?

3. Who can I speak with if I do not feel safe?

4. Are there support groups for children of alcoholics or drug abusers?

5. How can I let my parent or friend know that his or her addiction affects me?

6. How can I help my siblings understand and cope with our parent's addiction?

7. Will my parent be arrested for his or her alcohol or drug abuse?

8. Should I tell my friend's parents that I think he or she has an addiction to alcohol or drugs?

9. My friend's addiction is making it hard to stay friends. Should I end the relationship?

10. If my parent abuses drugs or alcohol, will I?

The Teen Health & Wellness Personal Story Project

Be part of the Teen Health & Wellness Personal Story Project and share your story about successfully dealing with or overcoming a challenge. If your story is accepted for online publication, it will be posted on the Teen Health & Wellness site and featured on its homepage. You will also receive a certificate of achievement from Rosen Publishing and a $25 gift certificate to Barnes & Noble or Chapters.

Sharing stories is a powerful way to connect with other people. By sharing your story, you can connect with others who are dealing with these challenges. Visit teenhealthandwellness.com/static/personalstoryproject to read other teens' stories and to submit your own.

Scan this QR code to go to the Personal Story Project homepage.

Glossary

abuse To use something improperly, regardless of the harmful consequences.

addicted Being dependent on a substance or an activity.

alcoholism Alcohol addiction or the behavior that results from alcohol dependency.

amphetamines Drugs that work on the nervous system to lift a depressive mood or suppress the appetite.

antibiotic A medication that attacks the bacteria that cause infectious diseases.

antidepressants Medications used to treat mood disorders such as depression.

autism A disorder marked by difficulties in verbal and non-verbal communication and social interaction.

blood alcohol content (BAC) The concentration of alcohol in a person's bloodstream, given as a percentage.

depression A disorder characterized by sadness, hopelessness, apathy, and loss of appetite and sleep.

driving under the influence (DUI) Driving while impaired by drugs or alcohol.

drug A substance that has a physiological effect and that is sometimes illegal and sometimes prescribed to treat an illness or disorder.

fetal alcohol spectrum disorder (FASD) A condition that is caused in a child when a mother consumes excessive alcohol while pregnant.

illicit Not authorized by the law or other sets of rules.

mental health The condition of a person's emotional, psychological, and social well-being.

metabolize To physically and chemically process a substance in the body.

post-traumatic stress disorder (PTSD) A mental health disorder that occurs in reaction to a shocking or dangerous event.

psychotherapy A method of working through mental health problems by talking with a trained therapist.

recovery A process used to treat a disorder or disease.

rehabilitation center A place where people with addictions to drugs or alcohol receive treatment.

relapse The return of the symptoms of a disease or disorder after a period of making progress.

suicide The act of taking one's life intentionally.

For More Information

Al-Anon/Alateen Family Groups
1600 Corporate Landing Parkway
Virginia Beach, VA 23454
(757) 563-1600

Al-Anon/Alateen Family Groups (Canada)
275 Slater Street, Suite 900
Ottawa, ON K1P 5H9
Canada
(613) 723-8484

Website: http://www.al-anon.alateen.org
Facebook: @AlateenWSO
Twitter: @Alateen_WSO
Instagram: @alateen_wso
Al-Anon provides organized meetings to let participants share their experiences with alcoholism, whether they are alcoholics themselves or have an alcoholic family member. Alateen is a group specifically for teens with one or more alcoholic parents.

Canadian Centre on Substance Abuse (CCSA)
75 Albert Street, Suite 500
Ottawa, ON K1P 5E7
Canada
(613) 235-4048
Website: http://www.ccsa.ca/Eng/Pages/default.aspx

Twitter: @CCSACanada
Created by Parliament, the CCSA addresses substance
use on a national level by synthesizing research and
data.

National Institute on Alcohol Abuse and Alcoholism
(NIAAA)
National Institutes of Health (NIH)
9000 Rockville Pike
Bethesda, MD 20892
(888) 696-4222
Website: https://www.niaaa.nih.gov
Twitter: @NIAAAnews
The NIAAA focuses on conducting research and
providing information on the diagnosis, prevention,
and treatment of alcohol-related challenges.
Resources include fact sheets on alcohol
consumption and alcohol use disorder.

National Institute on Drug Abuse (NIDA)
Office of Science Policy and Communications, Public
Information, and Liason Branch
6001 Executive Boulevard
Room 5213, MSC 9561
Bethesda, MD 20892-9561
(301) 443-1124
Website: https://www.drugabuse.gov
Facebook: @NIDANIH
Twitter: @NIDAnews
NIDA provides research, treatment information, and
educational material on topics related to drug abuse.

Partnership for Drug-Free Kids
352 Park Avenue South, 9th Floor
New York, NY 10010
(212) 922-1560
Website: http://drugfree.org
Facebook: @partnershipdrugfree
Twitter: @drugnews
Instagram: @thepartnership
Committed to helping families with addicted children,
    the Partnership for Drug-Free Kids provides
    recommendations for professionals, platforms to
    share stories, and actions for national advocacy.

Substance Abuse and Mental Health Services
    Administration
5600 Fishers Lane
Rockville, MD 20857
(877) 726-4727
Website: https://www.samhsa.gov
Facebook: @samhsa
Twitter: @samhsa.gov
This US Department of Health and Human Services
    agency addresses public health-related issues
    involving the effects of substance abuse and mental
    illnesses.

Teen Health and Wellness
29 East 21st Street
New York, NY 10010
(877) 381-6649
Website: http://www.teenhealthandwellness.com

App: Teen Hotlines

Teen Health and Wellness provides nonjudgmental, straightforward, curricular, and self-help support on topics such as diseases, drugs and alcohol, nutrition, mental health, suicide and bullying, green living, and LGBTQ issues. Its free Teen Hotlines app provides a concise list of hotlines, help lines, and information lines on the subjects that affect teens most.

Websites

Because of the changing nature of internet links, Rosen Publishing has developed an online list of websites related to the subject of this book. This site is updated regularly. Please use this link to access this list:

http://www.rosenlinks.com/TNV/Drugs

For Further Reading

Barnett, Robin. *Addict in the House: A No-Nonsense Family Guide Through Addiction & Recovery.* Oakland, CA: New Harbinger Publications, 2016.

Brezina, Corona. *Alcohol and Drug Offenses: Your Legal Rights* (Know Your Rights). New York, NY: Rosen Publishing, 2015.

Gottfried Hollander, Barbara. *Addiction: Understanding Brain Diseases and Disorders*. New York, NY: Rosen Publishing, 2012.

Hamilton, Tracy Brown. *I Am Addicted to Drugs. Now What?* (Teen Life 411). New York, NY: Rosen Publishing, 2017.

Hardy, Danielle. *Dealing with an Alcoholic Parent: A Child's Guide to an Alcoholic Parent*. Seattle, WA: CreateSpace Independent Publishing, 2016.

Henneberg, Susan. *Defeating Addiction and Alcoholism*. (Effective Survival Strategies). New York, NY: Rosen Publishing, 2016.

Leonard, Basia, and Jeremy Roberts. *The Truth About Prescription Drugs.* (Drugs and Consequences). New York, NY: Rosen Publishing, 2012.

Lew, Kristi. *The Truth About Oxycodone and Oher Narcotics.* (Drugs and Consequences). New York, NY: Rosen Publishing, 2014.

Meyer, Terry Teague. *I Have an Alcoholic Parent. Now What?* (Teen Life 411). New York,NY: Rosen Publishing, 2015.

Quinones, Sam. *Dreamland: The True Tale of America's*

Opiate Epidemic. London, UK: Bloomsbury Press, 2015.

Sheff, David. *Clean: Overcoming Addiction and Ending America's Greatest Tragedy*. New York, NY: Houghton Mifflin Harcourt Publishing: 2014.

Sheff, Nic. *We All Fall Down: Living with Addiction*. New York, NY: Hachette Book Group, 2012.

Spiegelman, Erica. *Rewired: A Bold New Approach to Addiction and Recovery*. New York, NY: Hatherleigh Press (Penguin Random House), 2015.

Szalavitz, Maia. *Unbroken Brain: A Revolutionary New Way of Understanding Addiction*. New York, NY: St. Martin's Press, 2016.

Bibliography

"Aden's Story." Teen Health and Wellness. June 2015.
http://www.teenhealthandwellness.com
/article/136/10/adens-story.

"Ben's Story." Teen Health and Wellness. December
2015. http://www.teenhealthandwellness.com
/article/293/9/bens-story.

Canadian Centre on Substance Abuse. "Substance Use
and Suicide Among Youth: Prevention and
Intervention Strategies." 2016. http://www.ccsa.ca
/Resource%20Library/CCSA-Substance-Use
-Suicide-Prevention-Youth-Summary-2016-en.pdf.

Centers for Disease Control and Prevention. "Drug
Overdose Deaths in the United States Continue to
Increase in 2015." December 16, 2016. https://www
.cdc.gov/drugoverdose/epidemic.

Chasnoff, Ira J. *The Mystery of Risk: Drugs, Alcohol,
Pregnancy, and the Vulnerable Child*. Portland, OR:
NTI Upstream, 2011.

"Jaquetta's Story." Teen Health and Wellness. June
2015. http://www.teenhealthandwellness.com
/article/37/12/jaquettas-story.

"Mercedes's Story." Teen Health and Wellness. June
2015. http://www.teenhealthandwellness.com
/article/131/12/mercedess-story.

"Michael's Story." Teen Health and Wellness. June 2015.
http://www.teenhealthandwellness.com/article/351/9
/michaels-story.

National Highway Traffic Safety Administration. "Drunk Driving." Retrieved February 2017. https://www.nhtsa.gov/risky-driving/drunk-driving.

Nemours Foundation: KidsHealth. "Fetal Alcohol Syndrome." August 2016. http://kidshealth.org/en/parents/fas.html.

"Preston's Story". Teen Health and Wellness. January 2016. http://www.teenhealthandwellness.com/article/129/9/prestons-story.

Searidge Foundation. "Characteristics and Personalities of Adults Who Grew Up with Alcoholism in the House." 2016. http://www.searidgealcoholrehab.com/article-adult-children-of-alcoholics.php.

"Tyler's Story." Teen Health and Wellness. June 2015. http://www.teenhealthandwellness.com/article/37/11/tylers-story.

US Department of Health and Human Services: Child Welfare Information Gateway. "Parental Substance Use and the Child Welfare System." October 2014. https://www.childwelfare.gov/pubPDFs/parentalsubabuse.pdf.

"Whitney's Story." Teen Health and Wellness. June 2015. http://www.teenhealthandwellness.com/article/37/10/whitneys-story.

"Zachary's Story." Teen Health and Wellness. June 2015. http://www.teenhealthandwellness.com/article/131/10/zacharys-story.

Index

A

abuse, 41
addiction
  children of someone with, 29
  cycle of, 8
  death caused by, 46
  in a friend, 17–19, 24–26
  hotlines, 44
  of a parent, 4–5, 23, 27, 30–33, 35–38, 40–41, 48
  and pregnancy, 4–5, 28, 48
  to prescription drugs, 46
  recovery from, 8, 18–19, 40, 48
  support groups, 19
  in teens, 5
Al-Anon, 8, 44
Alcoholics Anonymous (AA), 8
alcoholism, 4–5, 8, 27, 50
  in a friend, 17–19
  in a grandparent, 38–41
  in a parent, 30–33, 36–38, 41–45
antibiotics, 6
antidepressants, 30
anxiety disorders, 29, 30

B

babies born exposed to alcohol/drugs, 5
blood alcohol content (BAC), 9, 14

D

death of a parent, 22, 36–38
depression, 23, 29
divorce, 23
drug abuse, 6, 17–19, 48, 50
  difference from use, 6
  of prescription drugs, 6, 46
drug overdose, 46
drunk driving, 9, 15, 27
  death caused by, 9, 10
  driving under the influence (DUI) charge, 15, 16
  legal limit, 9
  statistics, 9, 16
  teens, 10, 11–15

E

enabling, 17

F

fetal alcohol spectrum disorder (FASD), 28, 49
fetal alcohol syndrome

About the Editor

Jennifer Landau is an author and editor who has written about psychological bullying, cybercitizenship, and drug and alcohol abuse, among other topics. She has a MA in English from New York University and an MST in general and special education from Fordham University. Landau has taught writing to young children, teens, and seniors.

About Dr. Jan

Dr. Jan Hittelman, a licensed psychologist with over thirty years experience working with children and families, has authored monthly columns for the *Daily Camera*, Boulder Valley School District, and online for Rosen Publishing Group. He is the founder of the Boulder Counseling Cooperative and the director of Boulder Psychological Services.

Photo Credits